TUNISIA TRAVEL GUIDE FOR BEGINNERS

The Updated Concise Guide for Planning a Trip to Tunisia Including Top Destinations,Culture,Outdoor Activities,Practical Tips and Getting Around

Thanh Minick
Copyright@2023

TABLE OF CONTENT

CHAPTER 1

INTRODUCTION

Situated on the Mediterranean coast of North Africa, Tunisia is a diverse destination that showcases a vibrant blend of historical significance, cultural heritage, and scenic landscapes. Tunisia, due to its advantageous geographical position that facilitates connections between Europe, Africa, and the Middle East, has served as a significant intersection of several civilizations throughout history. Consequently, this historical interaction has had a lasting impact on the country's landscapes and cultural practices. The purpose of this introduction is to provide a compelling synopsis of Tunisia, emphasizing its geographical characteristics, historical importance, and cultural assets that attract tourists from many parts of the world.

Geographical Marvels: An Exploration of Diverse Landscapes

The geographical appeal of Tunisia is extensive, presenting a wide array of vistas that captivate the mind. The northern shore of the nation is bordered by the blue Mediterranean Sea, which is known for its picturesque beaches and quaint coastal towns that emanate a tranquil atmosphere. As an individual embarks farther into the interior regions, the landscape undergoes a significant metamorphosis, characterized by the transition from undulating hills to the majestic Atlas Mountains situated in the western part. The mountains in question not only provide awe-inspiring panoramas, but also offer intrepid individuals the chance to traverse lush valleys and engage with the local indigenous Berber inhabitants of the area.

Continuing the journey in a southern direction unveils the captivating Sahara Desert, a renowned area characterized by its vast golden dunes that extend ceaselessly into the far horizon. The expansive desert terrain conceals ancient oasis, wherever life flourishes despite the harsh aridity. Visitors have the opportunity to partake in the enchantment of camel expeditions underneath the celestial expanse of the desert's starry night. The diverse geography of Tunisia caters to the preferences of many travelers, offering opportunities for leisure, adventure, and cultural immersion.

The subject of this discourse is to the intricate interweaving of historical events and cultural elements, resulting in a rich and diverse tapestry.

The historical importance of Tunisia might be likened to a complex tapestry, interwoven with elements from ancient civilizations and contemporary influences. The history of the nation may be traced back for thousands of years, as shown by the presence of architectural and monumental remnants from many civilizations like as the Phoenicians, Romans, Byzantines, and Arabs. The tactile manifestation of this cultural legacy is most evident at Carthage, the renowned historical metropolis that formerly had a comparable status to Rome and whose remnants still serve as a witness to the cyclical rise and fall of dominant civilizations.

The intricate network of streets of Tunis, the capital city, including the Medina of Tunis, which has been designated as a

UNESCO World Heritage site. The living museum showcases a plethora of elaborate architectural structures, vibrant marketplaces, and mosques that have stood the test of time, providing a glimpse into the essence of Tunisian culture. The Bardo National Museum in Tunisia is renowned for its extensive collection of Roman mosaics, which provide valuable insights into several aspects of ancient Roman culture, including mythology, everyday life, and opulence.

In this discourse, we explore the amalgamation of contemporary elements with traditional aspects.

Tunisia has a strong commitment to the preservation of its historical heritage, while also embracing the contemporary era and anticipating future developments. The streets of Sidi Bou Said, a picturesque beach community, are embellished with the distinctive blue and white architectural style that has become emblematic of the region's Mediterranean allure. Visitors have the opportunity to leisurely traverse the tight passageways, appreciating the harmonious juxtaposition of many hues and the fragrant aroma of jasmine that permeates the atmosphere.

The cultural richness of Tunisia extends beyond its architectural landmarks, including a vibrant culinary tradition that offers a captivating and immersive encounter. The culinary traditions of the nation showcase a harmonious amalgamation of Mediterranean, Arab, and Berber elements, yielding a diverse assortment of palatable delicacies. The culinary offerings of Tunisia showcase a diverse range of flavors that reflect the country's cultural richness. For instance, the substantial couscous, accompanied by succulent meats and vegetables, exemplifies this harmonic amalgamation. Similarly, the brik, a fried pastry generously packed with a delectable combination of egg and tuna, further exemplifies the fusion of tastes that characterize Tunisia's gastronomic landscape.

Tunisia transcends its status as a mere tourist destination, offering a profound sensory experience that spans both historical epochs and geographical dimensions. The interplay of geology, history, and culture in this region results in a captivating landscape that entices visitors to go into its lesser-known areas and indulge in its diverse range of encounters.

From the sun-drenched coastal areas in the north to the impressive sand dunes of the Sahara desert, each and every part of Tunisia's geographical features conveys a narrative. The ancient monuments of Carthage and the Medina of Tunis have the ability to transport tourists to bygone times characterized by magnificence and notable accomplishments. In the meanwhile, the contemporary liveliness of destinations such as Sidi Bou Said, together with the distinctive characteristics of its culinary offerings, accentuate the current appeal of the country.

Tunisia's diverse range of attractions caters to a variety of interests, including those of adventurous individuals, history enthusiasts, cultural aficionados, and those seeking relaxation by the seaside. This mosaic of goods ensures a voyage that is both intellectually stimulating and indelibly memorable. The North African region under consideration serves as a tangible representation of the lasting significance of human legacy and the limitless aesthetic appeal that emerges from the intersection of natural elements, historical events, and cultural expressions.

CHAPTER 2

Top Tourist Destinations

Tunisia, a nation with a rich historical background and a wide range of geographical features, offers several interesting locations that attract tourists due to its distinctive allure and historical importance. Tunisia's many destinations, including the vibrant streets of Tunis, the serene blue and white sanctuary of Sidi Bou Said, the golden beaches of Hammamet, and the enigmatic historical sites of Carthage, provide insights into the country's historical and contemporary aspects, as well as its captivating fusion of diverse cultures. This comprehensive investigation examines the prominent tourist attractions that contribute to Tunisia's appeal as a highly sought-after destination for those with a keen interest in history, aficionados of many cultures, and those in search of an indelible travel encounter.

1. Tunis: A Synthesis of Traditional and Contemporary Elements

Tunis, as the capital city, exhibits a dynamic atmosphere that effectively amalgamates contemporary elements with its rich historical legacy. The core of Tunis comprises the Medina, a monument recognized by UNESCO as a World Heritage site, which effectively immerses tourists in a historical period of the past. The medina's tiny passageways are adorned by souks, which serve as marketplaces that showcase a wide array of goods, ranging from spices and linens to exquisitely created ceramics and jewelry. The Great Mosque of Tunis, characterized by its distinctive minaret, serves as a tribute to the religious heritage and architectural magnificence of the city.

The Bardo National Museum, located inside the premises of a former palace, is an abundant repository of historical artifacts. The museum has a notable assemblage of Roman mosaics, renowned for their exceptional quality, which portray a wide range of subjects including mythological narratives, depictions of everyday activities, and significant historical occurrences. The museum furthermore provides a comprehensive understanding of Tunisia's multifaceted historical background, including its Carthaginian beginnings and the subsequent Arab and Islamic influences.

2. Sidi Bou Said: An Exemplary Whitewashed Haven

Situated on an elevated terrain with a commanding view of the Mediterranean Sea, Sidi Bou Said is a visually captivating hamlet renowned for its unique architectural style characterized by the prominent use of blue and white hues. The town's streets, characterized by their narrowness, are embellished with vibrant bougainvillea, creating an aesthetic reminiscent of a meticulously crafted artwork. The presence of Andalusian influence is evident in this location, as shown by the presence of elaborate entrances, wrought-iron window grilles, and peaceful courtyards, all of which contribute to the village's overall appeal.

The flourishing art culture of Sidi Bou Said serves as a tribute to the creative spirit that permeates the area. Tunis has a plethora of art galleries, studios, and craft stores, making it an ideal destination for the appreciation of local artistic prowess and the potential acquisition of distinctive Tunisian artwork.

Hammamet: A Fusion of Beaches and Culture

Hammamet is a seaside destination renowned for its picturesque landscape and diverse cultural offerings, providing visitors with an enchanting combination of abundant sunshine, pristine beaches, and rich heritage. The unspoiled coastal areas, characterized by their crystal-clear turquoise seas, serve as a magnet for those seeking sunbathing opportunities and engaging in other water-related activities. The town's contemporary appearance is enhanced by the presence of its old Medina of Hammamet, characterized by a complex network of tiny thoroughfares, whitewashed architectural structures, and vibrant marketplaces.

Hammamet is also home to a distinctive cultural monument known as the International Cultural Center. The aforementioned cultural institution serves as a platform for organizing various events, exhibits, and performances that aim to commemorate Tunisia's rich creative past and facilitate cross-cultural interactions on a global scale.

Djerba, an island located in the southern part of Tunisia, is renowned for its captivating allure and rich spiritual heritage.

Situated along the southern coast of Tunisia, the island of Djerba captivates visitors with its serene ambiance, picturesque beaches, and rich cultural legacy. The El Ghriba Synagogue in Djerba, Tunisia, is recognized as one of the most ancient Jewish synagogues globally, serving as a significant representation of the island's rich mixed heritage. Visitors are cordially invited to engage in the exploration of the architectural and cultural aspects of its interiors, so gaining insight into the profound interrelationships that exist among diverse religious groups.

In addition to its religious landmarks, the sceneries of Djerba include a diverse array of olive fields, palm palms, and picturesque towns. The island's inherent genuineness and unadorned nature make it an ideal sanctuary for those in pursuit of tranquility and respite from the frenetic pace of daily existence.

5. Matmata: Exploring Subterranean Realms Matmata, a unique destination, offers an intriguing opportunity to delve into the depths of underground realms.

Matmata is a captivating site that immerses guests in a surreal setting characterized by troglodyte homes. The subterranean dwellings discussed above were meticulously excavated into the pliable rock formations of the area, resulting in an intricate system of interconnected chambers and passageways that provide a sanctuary from the intense arid climate. Matmata has garnered global recognition due to its inclusion as one of the shooting sites for the renowned Star Wars saga, hence augmenting its appeal to aficionados of cinema and followers of the science fiction genre.

A visit to Matmata offers a unique chance to immerse oneself in a lifestyle that has endured with few alterations over the course of many centuries. The indigenous Berber populations in the area have successfully maintained their cultural traditions and lifestyle, providing an opportunity for tourists to get insight into a realm that is both historically significant and intriguingly strange.

The topic of discussion is Carthage: Echoes of Empires Past.

The ancient metropolis of Carthage serves as a witness to the cyclical nature of imperial ascension and decline, as well as the persistent fascination with the past. Carthage, established by the Phoenicians during the 9th century BC, saw significant growth and emerged as a formidable contender to Rome, ultimately becoming the focal point of a robust Mediterranean empire. Presently, the remnants of this site serve as a testament to a narrative encompassing the themes of military triumph, devastation, and the interchange of cultural influences.

The Carthage Archaeological Park has a collection of noteworthy artifacts, which include the Antonine Baths, the Punic Port, and the Roman Amphitheatre. The Punic Tophet, an archaic funerary site, provides valuable insights on the spiritual and religious customs observed by the Carthaginian civilization. Carthage, situated in a strategically advantageous location with a commanding view of the Gulf of Tunis, offers an opportunity for tourists to immerse themselves in the historical context and appreciate the magnificence of ancient civilizations.

Tunisia's greatest tourist sites include a diverse range of experiences that appeal to a broad spectrum of interests and curiosity. Each site in Tunisia, from the historically significant Carthage to the artistically vibrant Sidi Bou Said, has a fragment of the overall picture that represents the country. The nation's rich cultural legacy, varied geographical features, and hospitable towns provide a platform for tourists to embark on their own distinctive voyage. Tunisia's attractions provide an exceptional opportunity to see a nation where historical sites, picturesque beaches, and lively local markets converge, creating a harmonic blend of past, aesthetics, and contemporary elements.

CHAPTER 3

Cultural Experiences

Tunisia, a country situated in the Mediterranean region and renowned for its rich historical background, presents a diverse range of cultural encounters that captivate the senses and deeply engage visitors in its lively legacy. Tunisia beckons travelers to embark on a cultural expedition that seamlessly intertwines heritage and contemporary, including the indulgence in the enticing fragrances and tastes of its exquisite food, as well as the observation of the rhythmic cadences of its vibrant festivals. This study examines the core elements of Tunisia's cultural offerings, highlighting the gastronomy, festivals, events, and local markets that add to its appeal as a vibrant and diverse destination known for its authenticity.

Title: Cuisine: An Exquisite Culinary Experience Introduction: Cuisine, an art form that tantalizes the taste buds and delights the senses, is a subject of immense fascination and appreciation. This gastronomic

The culinary scene in Tunisia is characterized by a complex amalgamation of tastes that reflect the country's historical influences and diverse geographical features. Tunisian cuisine is a harmonious blend of flavors influenced by Mediterranean, Arab, Berber, and Ottoman culinary traditions.

Couscous, a much cherished dietary staple, may be regarded as a type of culinary art. The fine grains undergo a steaming process that results in an optimal texture, which harmonizes flawlessly with succulent meats, vegetables, and fragrant spices. The brik, a delectable pastry consisting of a crispy outer shell encasing a filling of egg, tuna, and capers, serves as a culinary representation of Tunisia's vibrant Mediterranean essence. Harissa, a piquant chili paste, imparts a potent spiciness to culinary preparations and serves as a prime illustration of the nation's affinity for assertive taste profiles.

The street food culture in Tunisia flourishes, providing a captivating chance to partake in regional delicacies. During the twilight hours, vibrant food vendors provide a variety of delicacies such as makbouba, a kind of fried bread filled with savory ingredients, merguez, which are sausages seasoned with aromatic spices, and marqa, flavorful soups that exemplify the essence of Tunisian gastronomy. Investigating the gastronomic landscape not only provides a sensory delight for the gustatory senses, but also offers a glimpse into the cultural heritage and communal ethos of the nation.

Festivals and events serve as a commemoration of the essence of existence.

Tunisia's calendar is marked by lively festivals and events that embody its exuberance for life and cultural diversity. The Carthage International Festival, an annual event hosted in the renowned city of Carthage, showcases a diverse range of cultural expressions including music, theater, dance, and visual arts from various parts of the globe. In the presence of historical remnants, artists and performers converge to create an ambiance characterized by artistic ingenuity and cultural interchange.

The Festival of the Sahara, which takes place at Douz, a location situated at the entrance of the Sahara Desert, is an event that commemorates Tunisia's nomadic legacy. This vibrant festival features camel racing, traditional music, and desert crafts, providing visitors with an opportunity to fully engage with the cultural practices of the country's desert-dwelling populations. The event serves as a testimony to the significance of preserving Tunisia's cultural heritage and disseminating it globally.

Local markets, also known as souks, play a significant role in showcasing and promoting traditional handicrafts. These markets serve as vibrant hubs where artisans and craftsmen display their well crafted products, reflecting the rich cultural heritage of the region. Sou

The act of exploring the local marketplaces, also known as souks, in Tunisia is a captivating sensory experience that serves as an introduction for travelers to the essence of Tunisian culture and the artistry of its people. The Medina marketplaces found in towns like as Tunis, Sousse, and Sfax provide a wide array of handcrafted products, ranging from elaborately crafted fabrics and carpets to delicately designed pottery and leather items. The market's historical significance as a center for commerce and cultural interchange is well conveyed via the lively hues, busy pathways, and animated negotiations, all of which contribute to a genuine experience. The Souk el Attarine in Tunis serves as a notable example, characterized by its labyrinthine corridors permeated with the fragrances of various spices, perfumes, and customary herbal treatments. The Souk des Teinturiers in Sousse, also known as the Dyers' Souk, serves as a platform for the exhibition of the traditional craft of cloth dyeing with organic colors. This time-honored technique has been transmitted over several generations. These markets provide not only a chance to purchase distinctive souvenirs but also an opportunity to interact with skilled craftsmen who safeguard Tunisia's traditional skills.

Embracing Culture: Practical Strategies for Cultural Integration

The cultural experiences offered in Tunisia are very enlightening; yet, it is important for tourists to exercise mindfulness about local conventions and decorum. Modesty in attire has significant cultural importance within the largely Muslim community, particularly while visiting holy locations. The act of dressing in a conservative manner, which entails covering one's shoulders and knees, is often seen as a gesture of respect and is held in high esteem.

Interacting with others from the local community in a respectful and considerate way cultivates significant interpersonal relationships. Acquiring a rudimentary understanding of fundamental Arabic words or salutations may significantly facilitate first social interactions and demonstrate a commendable regard for the indigenous cultural norms.

The topic of discussion pertains to sustainability and responsible tourism.

The integration of Tunisia's cultural
experiences is intricately linked with the
practice of responsible tourism. The act of
directly buying handcrafted items from
local craftsmen not only helps in sustaining
their livelihoods but also serves to preserve
traditional workmanship. Opting for
environmentally sustainable tours and
lodgings may contribute to the reduction of
environmental and socio-cultural impacts.

The cultural encounters in Tunisia include a
diverse array of tastes, sounds, and views,
which engender a deep feeling of
connection among tourists. The culinary
traditions, cultural celebrations, organized
gatherings, and community marketplaces
exemplify a country that values its
historical legacy while also eagerly
embracing the prospects of the future. By

engaging in these cultural interactions, tourists are not passive observers but rather active contributors to the vibrant fabric of Tunisian society, characterized by its variety and the lasting heritage of its inhabitants.

CHAPTER 4

Outdoor Activities

Tunisia, a country characterized by a variety of landscapes including unspoiled Mediterranean beaches and the expansive Sahara Desert, is an exceptional destination for those with a penchant for outdoor activities, providing them with an array of captivating natural scenery and thrilling experiences. Tunisia offers a diverse range of outdoor activities that appeal to the desires of travelers looking to experience its stunning scenery. These activities include exciting desert exploits as well as relaxing dips in the blue seas. This study examines the diverse range of outdoor activities available in Tunisia, including the exploration of the Sahara Desert, the Atlas Mountains, and the Mediterranean coast.

The Sahara Desert: An Enigmatic Landscape of Extraordinary Phenomena

The Sahara Desert, recognized as the biggest hot desert on Earth, serves as a remarkable manifestation of the formidable and captivating force inherent in the natural world. Engaging in a profound exploration of the central region of this extensive area entails embarking on a voyage into a transcendent domain characterized by expansive dunes of a golden hue that extend to the limits of visual perception. Desert trips provide adventurous individuals with the opportunity to navigate the captivating terrain by camel, traversing historical trade routes and immersing themselves in the unique seclusion that characterizes desert environments.

The coming of evening in the Sahara is regarded as one of the most captivating occasions. As the sun descends below the horizon, an expansive cosmic expanse emerges above, unveiling a resplendent exhibition of stars that seem to be within close proximity. The night sky of the Sahara, devoid of urban light pollution, provide as a captivating backdrop that showcases the rich narratives of past civilizations and the awe-inspiring phenomena of the cosmos.

The Atlas Mountains: A Prominent Destination for Adventurous Exploration and Intellectual Enlightenment

Located in the northwestern region of Tunisia, the Atlas Mountains provide a notable juxtaposition to the dry and barren desert terrains. The mountain range in question, spanning over the North African region, serves as a sanctuary for those with a penchant for outdoor activities such as climbing, trekking, and engaging in cultural experiences.

The hiking routes inside the Atlas Mountains provide an opportunity for individuals to engage in the exploration of the Berber settlements that are scattered across the challenging topography. The villages, characterized by the enduring presence of traditional lifestyles, provide a warm and hospitable welcome to guests. The visually appealing natural environments, including verdant valleys and rugged mountain summits, provide an aesthetically pleasing setting for unforgettable hiking experiences and a profound communion with the natural world.

The Mediterranean Coast: An Attractive Destination for Sun and Sea Recreation

The Mediterranean coastline of Tunisia is well regarded as an idyllic destination for those who like beaches and water-related activities. This region has picturesque coastal villages, pristine sandy shores, and captivating turquoise seas. The coastal areas of Hammamet, Sousse, and Djerba provide prospects for leisure and revitalization, where the melodic cadence of the ocean waves serves as a calming accompaniment to unhurried sunbathing and serene walks along the coastline.

The Mediterranean region provides a diverse range of aquatic activities for anyone seeking more physically engaging recreational endeavors. The activities of snorkeling and diving provide opportunities to explore and observe diverse and dynamic underwater ecosystems that are abundant with a wide variety of marine organisms and visually striking coral reefs. Windsurfing and kitesurfing use the coastal wind patterns to provide thrilling recreational activities and offer picturesque vistas of the shoreline.

Practical Guidelines for Engaging in Outdoor Expeditions

Participating in outdoor activities in Tunisia requires meticulous planning and adherence to environmental considerations and indigenous cultural norms. Outlined below are few pragmatic recommendations aimed at guaranteeing a secure and intellectually stimulating encounter:

The topic of weather awareness is of utmost importance. The climate in Tunisia exhibits significant variability, therefore necessitating a thorough understanding of the prevailing weather patterns in the specific locale one intends to visit. The Sahara Desert exhibits significant diurnal temperature variations, with scorching daytime heat and unexpectedly cold nighttime conditions. It is advisable to bring appropriate clothing and supplies to accommodate these high temperature fluctuations.

2. The Importance of Sun Protection: The solar radiation in North Africa is known for its high intensity. It is advisable to consistently apply sunscreen, use a wide-brimmed hat, and don lightweight, long-sleeved attire as precautionary measures against the harmful effects of sunburn.

The topic of hydration will be discussed in this section. Maintaining proper hydration is of utmost importance, particularly in arid regions. It is essential to ensure that a sufficient quantity of water is carried and constantly replenished.

4. It is important to demonstrate respect for local customs and traditions while participating in outdoor activities in close proximity to communities or cultural places. It is advisable to adhere to modest attire, particularly in regions characterized by traditional cultural norms.

5. Guided Tours: It is advisable to contemplate the option of participating in guided tours for engaging in activities such as desert treks or mountain climbs. Local guides play a crucial role in offering

significant perspectives, bolstering safety measures, and making substantial contributions to the local economy.

The topic of sustainability and responsible exploration is of great importance in academic discourse.

Responsible tourism practices are of utmost importance in any outdoor excursion. By adopting practices that reduce their environmental footprint, demonstrating cultural sensitivity, and following to the principles of Leave No Trace, individuals may contribute to the long-term preservation of Tunisia's natural wonders for future generations.

Tunisia's range of outdoor activities caters to those seeking excitement as well as those with a deep appreciation for the natural world. Tunisia's diverse landscapes, ranging from the enchanting Sahara Desert to the majestic Atlas Mountains and the captivating Mediterranean coast, provide an irresistible invitation for tourists to engage in exploration, discovery, and a profound connection with the natural marvels of our planet. The nation's wide range of outdoor attractions serves as evidence of its notable geographical and cultural variety, enticing travelers to participate in expeditions that enhance their spiritual well-being and forge enduring recollections among the splendor of the natural world.

CHAPTER 5

Practical Tips

Embarking upon a voyage to Tunisia, a nation rich in historical, cultural, and natural wealth, requires a combination of eager expectation and meticulous planning. This thorough book provides practical recommendations to enhance your travel experience in this interesting North African country, covering aspects such as knowing local traditions and ensuring a flawless journey.

One of the key aspects to consider while traveling internationally is the visa and entry requirements. Commence with the fundamental principles.

Prior to embarking on a journey to Tunisia, it is important to get a comprehensive understanding of the visa prerequisites and entrance laws that pertain to individuals of your specific nationality. It is advisable to consult the Tunisian embassy or consulate in your respective country in order to get precise and current information pertaining to visa applications and the necessary papers. It is advisable to engage in proactive planning in order to mitigate any potential inconveniences and delays that may arise upon arrival.

2. Optimal Timing for Visiting: Customizing Your Travel Experience

The temperature in Tunisia exhibits variation, so the date of one's visit may have a substantial influence on their overall experience. The optimal timing for travel is contingent upon one's own interests and preferred activities. The months of spring (March to May) and autumn (September to

November) provide favorable climatic conditions for the exploration of historical landmarks, participation in outdoor recreational pursuits, and the appreciation of coastal landscapes. Summers in some places, particularly desert areas, are characterized by high temperatures, whilst winters are comparatively cooler and provide favorable conditions for engaging in tourism activities inside urban centers and coastal zones.

3. An Analysis of Currency Exchange and its Significance in Financial Transactions

The designated monetary unit of Tunisia is the Tunisian Dinar (TND). It is advisable to convert a portion of currency upon arrival at the airport or in prominent urban centers. Although credit cards are often accepted in hotels, restaurants, and bigger retail businesses, it is recommended to have cash on hand for smaller enterprises, local markets, and gratuities. Automated Teller Machines (ATMs) are widely accessible in metropolitan regions, facilitating easy transactions for those seeking to withdraw cash.

4. Health and Safety: Placing Emphasis on Personal Well-being

Health measures are of utmost importance while embarking on a journey. It is advisable to seek consultation with a medical practitioner or a specialist in travel health sufficiently in advance of your planned journey in order to engage in a comprehensive discussion on vaccines, medicines, and any pertinent health issues. It is advisable to own a rudimentary first aid pack with fundamental items such as analgesics, disinfectants, and dressings.

Tunisia is usually considered to be a safe place for tourists; nonetheless, like with any location, it is advisable to exercise care and implement necessary safety measures. It is essential to be well-informed on local news and ongoing happenings, while also maintaining a heightened sense of awareness regarding one's immediate environment. It is advisable to refrain from overtly exhibiting important possessions and to ensure the security of personal things, particularly in densely populated environments.

5. Language and Communication: Bridging the Gap In this section, we will explore the topic of language and communication and

how it serves as a bridge to connect individuals and communities.

Arabic serves as the designated official language of Tunisia, however English and French are extensively spoken, particularly within tourist regions, hotels, and commercial establishments. Acquiring a rudimentary understanding of Arabic expressions or using a translation application may augment one's engagement with indigenous people and exhibit appreciation for their culture.

6. Transportation: Navigating the Surroundings

The ease of navigating Tunisia is facilitated by its efficient and interconnected transportation infrastructure. The following are many prominent transportation alternatives:

Taxis, a kind of transportation, are often used by individuals to get from one location to another. Taxis are a prevalent means of transportation inside urban areas. It is advisable to ensure the use of the taxi meter or establish a mutually agreed-upon fee prior to commencing your travel.

Public transportation systems, such as buses and railways, serve as vital means of connectivity between large urban centers and smaller municipalities. The railway system exhibits a commendable level of efficiency and comfort, providing a picturesque means of transportation for traversing between various places.

Car rentals are a service provided by companies that allow individuals to temporarily lease a vehicle for a certain period of time. In the event that one intends to go outside metropolitan regions, the option of renting an automobile might provide more adaptability. It is important to possess an international driving permit and adequately anticipate diverse road circumstances.

7. Cultural Etiquette: Observance of Local Customs In order to foster positive interactions and avoid cultural misunderstandings, it is essential to demonstrate respect for the customs and traditions of the local culture.

The comprehension and appreciation of indigenous cultures are important in fostering a favorable trip encounter. In the context of Tunisia, there is a cultural value placed on the practice of dressing modestly, particularly while engaging in visits to sacred places. It is advisable for women to contemplate the option of having a scarf with them, which may be used to cover their shoulders as and when required. It is advisable to limit public expressions of love.

It is traditional to remove one's shoes while entering houses or mosques. The act of greeting someone by a handshake is widely observed, while the practice of addressing them with the word salam (which translates to peace) is considered a kind gesture.

8. Photography and Permissions: Ethical Approaches to Documenting Memories

The photographic opportunities in Tunisia's lively settings are quite appealing; yet, it is essential to demonstrate due regard for indigenous traditions and personal boundaries. It is essential to always get permission before to capturing photographs of individuals, particularly in rural regions. It is advisable to ascertain the rules and signage pertaining to photographing at historical places, since some limitations may be in place.

9. Regional Gastronomy: Indulging in Culinary Delights

The culinary offerings of Tunisia are a notable aspect of every journey. Embrace the indigenous culinary offerings and engage in the exploration of classic gastronomic delicacies like as couscous, brik, and tajine. Street food is an essential experience that provides an opportunity to savor the genuine flavors of the local culture. It is important to prioritize adherence to hygiene protocols, particularly by adhering to established standards. It is advisable to opt for the use of bottled water for both drinking and oral hygiene practices such as tooth brushing.

10. The Significance of Sustainable Tourism in Generating Positive Outcomes

The preservation of Tunisia's natural and cultural assets is contingent upon the practice of responsible travel. It is important to exercise environmental consciousness by adopting practices that minimize plastic use, promote water conservation, and ensure responsible trash disposal. One way to promote the local economy is by actively engaging in the purchase of handcrafted items, so supporting local craftsmen.

In summary, Tunisia offers a diverse array of experiences that appeal to a broad spectrum of interests. By adhering to these pragmatic suggestions, individuals will be adequately equipped to engage with the historical, cultural, and environmental aspects of the nation, all the while effectively managing the complexities associated with everyday existence. It is important to bear in mind that every voyage presents a unique chance to engage with a distinct culture, broaden one's perspectives, and create enduring memories in this captivating North African locale.

THE END

Made in the USA
Las Vegas, NV
17 March 2024

87346681R00036